# Kingdom Verses

RHODA BENJAMIN

Printed in the United States of America.

Library of Congress Control Number: 2019915162

ISBN          Paperback          978-1-64803-531-9
              Hardback           978-1-64803-532-6
              eBook              978-1-64803-533-3

**Westwood Books Publishing LLC**
11416 SW Aventino Drive
Port Saint Lucie, FL 34987

www.westwoodbookspublishing.com

# Contents

# Introduction

"Who hath delivered us from the power of darkness, and hath translated us into the kingdom of his dear Son" (Colossians 1:13).

---

As I compile this collection of poems – Kingdom Verses, my desire is that it will bring comfort and hope to us in the midst of human hopelessness, spiritual direction to lead us into a deeper relationship with Jesus Christ, and courage as we await the second coming of Christ.

Kingdom Verses, reminds us that Jesus is the only true solution to our problems, for He said "The thief cometh not, but for to steal, and to kill, and to destroy: I am come that they might have life, and that they might have it more abundantly" John 10:10.

Despite the daily battles that confront us, especially in our globalized and urban contexts, God reminds us in Jeremiah 29:11, that He is aware of the trials and challenges that we experience; that His thoughts towards us are that of peace, not evil, and to give us a bright future, a future of hope. God's Kingdom is an inner reality as He rules our hearts and minds by faith (Luke 17:21, Col 1:13). His Kingdom is also an outer reality (Matthew 6:10), as He enables us to live out the values of His Kingdom by the power of His Holy Spirit wherever we are, in anticipation of the world to come.

May Kingdom Verses help you reach out and grasp God's promises so that you may live hope-filled lives in this world, and in expectation of living life to the full in the world to come. We are faced with the realization that "If in this world only we have hope in Christ Jesus, we are of all men most miserable," 1 Corinthians 15:19.

I sincerely desire that this book "Kingdom Verses" will offer you hope, peace, and purpose in this troubled world. Above all be assured that God's plans for you are to give you a future with Him forevermore in the earth made new.

Kingdom Sister,
Rhoda Benjamin
So what I say unto you, I say unto all, "Be faithful citizens of His Kingdom".

# Sauteurs, My Church, My Home

Welcome to Sauteurs, My Church, My Home
No Other Place I Could Call My Own
A Fortress of Love Surrounded by Stone
Like A City On A Hill Where Its Light Has Shone
A Mother Of Churches From Which Others Have Grown
That Is Sauteurs, My Church, My Home

I Remember The Days With Its Stalwart Elders
Brother Charles, Brother George, Brother Bhola, Many Others
Teachers Of Sound Doctrine, Champions Of The Faith
Knowledgeable In Scripture, Ellen White Took Second Place
Without Them To Stand In The Place Of The Pastor
Sauteurs Could Not Have Gone On, Conquering And To Conquer

The Youth of Sauteurs, What A Fine Group She Nurtured
Young Men And Women Who Were Dedicated And Committed Leaders
Sharon Moses With Her Majestic Youth Choir
With Stan Singing Bass, A Beautiful Voice From Anna
Dexter Thomas, An Exemplary Young Man
Sadly Taken From Us, Just In His Prime

Welcome To Sauteurs, My Church, My Home
This Beautiful Edifice, A Stature Of Stone
Early Sunday Mornings, We Gathered By The River
Collecting Stones And Having Fun With Each Other

Young And Old It Did Not Matter
Males and Females Joined Hands And Worked Together
I Salute You, Sauteurs, My Church, My Home
No Other Church I Could Call My Own
Commissioned By God To Preach Salvation
Proclaim Liberty, Justice, Christ's Second Visitation
Appointed To Be A Comforter To Those Who Mourn
And Ease The Pain Of Those Who Groan

And When We Would Have Returned To Canada, England, America,
Africa, Europe, And Wherever We Roam
We Would Still Remember Sauteurs, Our Church, Our Home
Because There's No Other Place We Could Call Our Own
So Welcome, One, Welcome, All
Welcome To Sauteurs! My Church, Your Church, Our Own!

# If My Religion

If my religion generates in me
Fear and anxiety, despondency, uncertainty
I will not practice it or share it
But confront it and dissociate myself from it

If my religion makes me feel
Distressed, depressed, demoralized, dehumanized
I will not practice it or share it
But reconsider it and shun it

If my religion supports me to be
Argumentative, confrontative, insensitive, impulsive
I will not practice it or share it
But be cautious of it and avoid it

If my religion causes me to be
Boastful, slothful, lustful, hateful
I will not practice it or share it
But despise it and run from it

If my religion allows me to become
Selfish, materialistic, inconsiderate, egotistic
I will not practice it or share it
But reject it and withdraw from it

If my religion desensitizes me to become
Cold and callous, proud, and pompous
Iwill not practice it or share it
But deny it and forsake it

If my religion perpetrates in me
Dishonesty, promiscuity, cruelty, inhumanity
I will not practice it or share it
But detest it and denounce it

If my religion drives me to become
Legalistic, dogmatic, chauvinistic, narcissistic
I will not practice it or share it
But abandon it and not recommend it

If my religion degrades me to the point, I'm no longer able
To differentiate between good and evil, right from wrong
I will not practice it or share it
I will very well sever connection with it, not consent to it

If my religion hypnotizes me to become so heavenly minded
That I am of no earthly good to anyone, including myself
I will not practice it or share it
I'll be compelled to re-examine it, to rethink it, to oppose it and abandon it

If my religion exalts me to the extent that
My personal opinions and philosophy replace the Holy Word of God
Then I'm setting myself up as God
I'm challenging the authority of God
I'm violating The Commandments of God

Oh! but if my religion promotes Jesus as the Solid Rock of Salvation
That leads me to repentance, obedience, conversion, transformation
That makes me loving, caring, forgiving
That enables me to be joyful, peaceful, hopeful, helpful
That empowers me to be Truthful, trustful
Thankful, faithful
I will apply it!
I'll believe it, I'll cherish it
I'll embrace it, I'll follow it
I'll practice it, I'll recommend it
I'll teach it, I'll be zealous about it
I will not keep it to myself
I cannot keep it to myself!
I'll definitely share it
I'll tell
The world about it!
I'll be willing
To die for it!
My religion?
Yes! My Religion

# Just Spinning

Spinning Like A Top In The Mud
Spinning, Just Spinning
Still Sitting There
Having Done Nothing
Go For A Walk, Do Something
It's High Time To Stop Procrastinating
Been Going Round And Round
Like A Wheel Stuck In The Mud
Spinning, Just Spinning
Going Nowhere, Achieving Nothing
Ambition Without Motivation
Continuous Procrastination
Indecision
Stuck, Yes, Stuck
Spinning
Sometimes Fast And Getting Faster
Sometimes Slow, Getting Slower
Moving But Not Going Anywhere
Spinning, Spinning, More Spinning
Just Spinning
Going Round And Round
Getting Nowhere, Achieving Nothing
Failing To Reach The Full Potential
That Sense Of Self-Actualization
But The Years Keep Going On And On!
Still Dreaming

But Having Done Nothing
To Follow The Dream
Except Spinning, Spinning,
More Spinning!

# Strive To Be

Strive To Be Beautiful, Faithful, And Peaceful
Strive To Be Trustful, Respectful, And Merciful
Strive To Be Forgiving, Loving, Longsuffering
Strive To Be Law-abiding, Understanding, God-fearing

Strive To Be Ambitious, Conscientious, Studious
Strive To Be Joyous, Generous, Courageous
Strive To Be True, Mature, And Pure
Strive To Persevere, Be Gentle, Feel Secure

Strive To Be Diligent, Resilient, Consistent
Strive To Be Transparent, Benevolent, Intelligent
Strive To Be Free From Hate, Accurate, And Temperate
Strive To Be Compassionate, Affectionate, And Not Try To Frustrate

Strive To Reflect The Image Of God
Strive To Be Like Him!

# *Shackl*

Take These Shackles Off, Take Then
Jesus Paid The Price In Full, It's Not
A Life Of Freedom and Honor Is Me
Stop Drinking, Smoking, Sitting Idl
Lying, Stealing, Taking Bribes To M
So! Take These Shackles Off, Take T

Take These Shackles Off, Take Then
Indulging In Pride, Mischief, And D
Sowing Discord, Shedding Innocent
Coveting, Cheating, Grabbing What
Remember All Of These Things The
Go! Remind The Devil He Faces Ete

Take These Shackles Off, Take Then
Be A Good Role Model, Work Hard,
Educate Yourself, Be Honest, Be Dis
Stand For Integrity, Be Diligent, Get
And Keep The Shackles Off, Keep T
Replace Them With Good Shoes, Sh

# Born to Win

I am not ashamed of my identity, a black woman, British born,
West Indian strong, naturalized American, legalized
I am created in the very image of God, benevolent, intelligent, gracious
Industrious, virtuous, religious—in God I trust
I have equal opportunity to be educated to whatever I wish to become
I am not dumb
I work, I play, I speak and say what I have to say
I do not have to succumb to the social injustice, the secular beliefs and
Immoral practices of this modern day
I have the clarity of mind to think coherently
Constructively, creatively, critically
I do not have to be a reflector of other men's thoughts because I am
unique

I am unique, I have rights!
Rights to exercise autonomy
Rights to advocate for the poor and disadvantaged in our society
Rights to sympathize with those who are incarcerated for crimes
With greater penalty for blacks and the minority
Rights to protest against the disregard for human life
And human dignity, because you see
My life matters, every life matters
I'm entitled to rights to equal access to God's gifts to humanity and the
Right to be free to be me
Right to be free to be me
Right to be free to be me!

I am born to win!
Not to be marginalized by racism, my religion
Or because I'm a woman
Neither to experience discrimination
Because of my skin pigmentation, my anatomical construction
Or because of some psychological dysfunction
Or physical debilitation
I am God's creation
I'm born to win!

I am born to win!
I will not be distracted by political propaganda
Or entertain irrational thoughts about security in America
And the Mexican border
God is my Protector
I'm born to win!

I am born to win!
I will not be preoccupied with anxiety and fears
Or depressive thoughts to make me shed tears
God sees and hears
He answers prayers
I'm born to win!

I am born to win!
I will not be alarmed about, facing the future
With the transfer of power from Barack Obama
With the rise of Trump Tower
Egomania, selective amnesia, and suppression of the media
The rich getting richer, the poor getting poorer
With America and Russia befriending each other
With threats of nuclear war from North Korea
With church and state colluding together
For the passing of the universal Sunday Law

# Strive To Be

Strive To Be Beautiful, Faithful, And Peaceful
Strive To Be Trustful, Respectful, And Merciful
Strive To Be Forgiving, Loving, Longsuffering
Strive To Be Law-abiding, Understanding, God-fearing

Strive To Be Ambitious, Conscientious, Studious
Strive To Be Joyous, Generous, Courageous
Strive To Be True, Mature, And Pure
Strive To Persevere, Be Gentle, Feel Secure

Strive To Be Diligent, Resilient, Consistent
Strive To Be Transparent, Benevolent, Intelligent
Strive To Be Free From Hate, Accurate, And Temperate
Strive To Be Compassionate, Affectionate, And Not Try To Frustrate

Strive To Reflect The Image Of God
Strive To Be Like Him!

# Shackles Off

Take These Shackles Off, Take Them Off Your Feet
Jesus Paid The Price In Full, It's Not A Secret
A Life Of Freedom and Honor Is Meant To Be Nice And Sweet
Stop Drinking, Smoking, Sitting Idly In The Street
Lying, Stealing, Taking Bribes To Make Ends Meet
So! Take These Shackles Off, Take Them Off Your Feet

Take These Shackles Off, Take Them Off Your Feet
Indulging In Pride, Mischief, And Deceit
Sowing Discord, Shedding Innocent Blood, Harboring Hate
Coveting, Cheating, Grabbing Whatever You Can Get
Remember All Of These Things The Good Lord Hates
Go! Remind The Devil He Faces Eternal Defeat

Take These Shackles Off, Take Them Off Your Feet
Be A Good Role Model, Work Hard, Put Some Shoes On Your Feet
Educate Yourself, Be Honest, Be Discreet
Stand For Integrity, Be Diligent, Get Off The Street
And Keep The Shackles Off, Keep Them Off Your Feet
Replace Them With Good Shoes, Shoes That Comfortably Fit

# Born to Win

I am not ashamed of my identity, a black woman, British born,
West Indian strong, naturalized American, legalized
I am created in the very image of God, benevolent, intelligent, gracious
Industrious, virtuous, religious—in God I trust
I have equal opportunity to be educated to whatever I wish to become
I am not dumb
I work, I play, I speak and say what I have to say
I do not have to succumb to the social injustice, the secular beliefs and
Immoral practices of this modern day
I have the clarity of mind to think coherently
Constructively, creatively, critically
I do not have to be a reflector of other men's thoughts because I am
unique

I am unique, I have rights!
Rights to exercise autonomy
Rights to advocate for the poor and disadvantaged in our society
Rights to sympathize with those who are incarcerated for crimes
With greater penalty for blacks and the minority
Rights to protest against the disregard for human life
And human dignity, because you see
My life matters, every life matters
I'm entitled to rights to equal access to God's gifts to humanity and the
Right to be free to be me
Right to be free to be me
Right to be free to be me!

I am born to win!
Not to be marginalized by racism, my religion
Or because I'm a woman
Neither to experience discrimination
Because of my skin pigmentation, my anatomical construction
Or because of some psychological dysfunction
Or physical debilitation
I am God's creation
I'm born to win!

I am born to win!
I will not be distracted by political propaganda
Or entertain irrational thoughts about security in America
And the Mexican border
God is my Protector
I'm born to win!

I am born to win!
I will not be preoccupied with anxiety and fears
Or depressive thoughts to make me shed tears
God sees and hears
He answers prayers
I'm born to win!

I am born to win!
I will not be alarmed about, facing the future
With the transfer of power from Barack Obama
With the rise of Trump Tower
Egomania, selective amnesia, and suppression of the media
The rich getting richer, the poor getting poorer
With America and Russia befriending each other
With threats of nuclear war from North Korea
With church and state colluding together
For the passing of the universal Sunday Law

With friends and neighbors betraying each other
Right here in Huntsville, Alabama
God, help us! My sister, my brother
But God is my Anchor, my Savior, my Deliverer
I will trust Him
I'm born to win!
I am born to win!
I'm a wife, a mother, a sister, a daughter
I sing, I pray, I feel God's anointing with each passing day
In God's holy eyes, I'm a pearl of infinite price
Christ died for my sin, I am destined to win!

I am born to win!
I'm so precious in the sight of God
That He left the very throne room of grace
To rescue me from the demise of the human race
Oh, what sacrifice
I'm born to win!

I am born to win!
I'm the daughter of a King
You are children of the King
You are born to win
I am born to win
We are born to win
We are children of the King
So rejoice! Let's sing!

STOP

# *Stop*

Stop! Go No Further
The Light Is On Red
To Cross Over Means Danger
You Can't Run Forever Because You Are Clever
Don't Be Enticed By The Devil, Lucifer
So Stop! Go No Further

Stop! The Odds Are Against You
Law Enforcement Officers Are Looking For You
Hiding, Hijacking, And Threatening Won't Save You
You Can't Run Forever
You Need To Surrender
So Stop! Go No Further

Stop! Stop!
The Red Light Is Flashing
This Means Danger! Your Final Warning
Now's The Time To Surrender
It's Now Or Never
Sorry, My Brother; Too Late! Your Life Is Over

Sad! Sad! You Thought You Were Clever
You Constantly Ignored The Voice Of Your Savior
What Lies Ahead Now, Is Facing Hell's Fire
Missed Opportunity To Live In Heaven Forever
Because You Thought You Were Young And Clever

Warning! Red Light Flashing
Today, If You Hear God's Voice, Harden Not Your Heart!

# Go! Sin No More

Go! And Sin No More
You're Forgiven, Made Clean And Pure
Been Reminded Several Times Before
When God Forgives, He Remembers No More

Go! And Sin No More
Temptation And Trials Will Help You Grow
Been Delivered From The Defeated Foe
But Resolve In Your Mind To Sin No More

Go! And Sin No More
Lucifer That Serpent Will Accuse You For Sure
Remember God's Promises Are Very Sure
Your Sins Are Forgiven, Salvation Secure

Go! And Sin No More
Jesus Is The Door
Through Which You Must Go
If You Hope To Live Forevermore

So Go! And Sin No More
Go! And Sin No More
Go! And Sin No More
Go!

# Happiness

It Cannot Be Bought
It Cannot Be Sold
It Is More Precious Than The Finest Gold
Happiness Is Beyond Description
With Overwhelming Feelings Of Gratification

Happiness Is A Treasured Gift
Without A Trace Of Envy Or Grief
Tell Me, Where Can It Be Found?
There, In The Word Of God It's Bound

In Your Pursuit Of Happiness
You Will Lower Your Blood Pressure, Alleviate Your Stress
But There Is One Thing You Must Surely Do
To Make Your Life's Aspirations Come True

So, One And All, I Appeal To You
You Want To Be Happy, Don't You?
Well, To Obtain The Happiness You Desire
Accept Jesus Christ As Your Personal Savior.

# *Here I Stand*

"Finally, be strong in the Lord and in his great power. Put on the full armor of God so that you can fight against the devil's evil tricks. Our fight is not against people on earth but against the rulers and authorities and the powers of this world's darkness, against the spiritual powers of evil in the heavenly world. That is why you need to put on God's full armor. Then on the day of evil you will be able to stand strong. And when you have finished the whole fight, you will still be standing." (Eph. 6:10–13, NCV).

And so, brothers and sisters
Here I stand, to take my stand
I will take my stand despite my thought blocks and memory gaps
My imperfect vision and sleep deprivation
My impatience, frustration, and human indignation
But with my freedom of choice and monotonic voice
I will take my stand to put aside my judgmental attitude
Show more grace, compassion, and express more gratitude
Bind up the broken hearted and proclaim deliverance to the captives
Comfort those who mourn and open the prison, to those who are bound
Bound by the chains of opioid and alcohol addiction
Food and fashion addiction
IPhone and Twitter addiction
Porn and TV addiction
Debt and credit card suffocation
Obsessive compulsion, depression, and suicidal ideation

Here I stand to take my stand
I will take my stand
To be sensitive to the needs of those around
To embrace all peoples, irrespective of race and religion
Social and economic situation, education, and sexual orientation
I will take my stand to stand against hatred and hostility
Bigotry and white supremacy
Nepotism and racism, sexism and ageism
I will take my stand against injustice, dehumanization, and corruption
Against abuse of the elderly and the mentally ill
Against domestic violence and gun violence
I will take my stand against oppression and segregation
Alienation and isolation in our institutions
I will safeguard against social media obsession and a legalistic religion
To not entertain selective amnesia and phobia of the media
To not indulge in narcissism, egocentrism, and need for recognition

Here I stand to take my stand
I will take my stand
Hand in hand with the Almighty, Omnipotent
Omniscient, Omnipresent God
Who challenges me
To hold on and move on
To press on and fight on
To live on and dream on
And take my stand
In a world that is groaning under the weight
Of guilt and shame, disease and pain
Headache and measles outbreak
Earthquake and heartbreak
Famine and flood
The shedding of blood
Immorality and infidelity
Idolatry and human ideology

Gender confusion and sexual perversion
Materialism and threat to religious freedom
Ethnic cleansing and human trafficking
Global warming with fire raging
Snow piling, and tornado blasting
Here I stand to take my stand
In these challenging times
I will take my stand and not be afraid to call sin by its rightful name
I will take my stand against spiritual complacency and mediocrity
I will take my stand against injustice and corruption
I will take my stand against sexual predators in high places and low places
In the White House and the School House
In the Play House and the Entertainment House
In the Court House and the Corporate House
In the House of Representatives, and the House of God
I will take my stand against misogyny in God's remnant church
Against power struggle, hypocrisy, and autocratic ideology
Against exploitation and misappropriation in our schools and institutions
Against those inflicting human pain
While upholding archaic traditions for selfish gains

Here I stand to take my stand
I will take my stand in this Land of Liberty
Where certain politicians surrender decency, integrity, and dignity
On the altar of sacrifice, in favor of loyalty to their political party
Where obstruction of justice is encountered in high places
Where truth is no longer held in high esteem by some in leadership positions
Where alternative facts seem to have become the norm
Making it difficult to differentiate between right and wrong
Where wrong doing is rationalized and presented as acceptable behavior
Where corruption and lies have become an integral part

Of the governing culture
Where greed and accumulation of wealth take priority
While millions suffer in poverty and experience health care disparity

Here I stand to take my stand
I will take my stand like Queen Esther and Tamar
Ruth and Mary, mother of Jesus Our Savior
Ellen White, Harriet Tubman, Rosa Parks, and Mother Teresa
Winnie Mandela and Michelle Obama
And though I may face the lion's den
Be confined to a prison cell or cast in a dark dungeon
And even if I go through the Valley of the shadow of death
I pray God to help me to stand strong and hold on
Until that day, when, along with those who have fought the good fight
We will stand together, irrespective of race or color
And resound songs of liberation
From every tribe and nation
Worshipping the God of our salvation
From Genesis to Revelation
Brothers and sisters
Take your stand
And stand!

$$\text{---}\ \infty\text{-}\circ\text{e}\text{r}\circ\text{-}\circ\text{t}\circ\text{e}\circ\circ\text{-}\text{vr}\ \text{---}$$

# The Upper Room

"Then they went back to Jerusalem from the Mount of Olives. (This mountain is about half a mile from Jerusalem.) When they entered the city, they went to the upstairs room where they were staying. Peter, John, James, Andrew, Philip, Thomas, Bartholomew, Matthew, James son of Alphaeus, Simon (known as the Zealot), and Judas son of James were there. They all continued praying together with some women, including Mary the mother of Jesus, and Jesus' brothers." (Acts 1:12–14, NCV).

An email was sent to my daughter, Esther, at Boston University, one day
At that time she was looking for a place to stay
Looking to find a room somewhere
The email read like this:
"A lovely loft-type room, available for rent, in our home
It is fully furnished, extremely spacious
It has a newly built private bath
Has cable, Wi-Fi and internet
There is a 40" television in the great sitting area, a microwave, and refrigerator
It is a must see! It includes utility."

I saw pictures of the room
It was a beautiful room, an attractive, clean, and spacious room
It looked like a warm and welcoming room, a quiet and comfortable room
It seemed like the sort of room where angels would love to tarry

And the Holy Spirit, not wanting to leave in a hurry
I liked the room; the Loft-Type room
It reminded me of The Upper Room where the followers of Jesus
Gathered to pray
To worship and fellowship, after Christ ascended into heaven on that
Historic day.

I went on my knees and prayed. I prayed and said to God,
"God, if this is going to be the room, then
Take the keys, unlock the door, and enter the room
Inspect the room and survey the room
Open up the curtains and allow sunshine from heaven to invade the
room
Let your Spirit ventilate the room
And circulate sweet fragrance inside the room
Deposit blessings from the windows of heaven and secure the room
Remodel the room and let peace like a river flow through the room
Then send holy angels to encamp around the room."

I said, "Lord, if it is that room, then
Let worship to God be given inside that room
Let Scriptures be studied inside that room
Let prayers be heard coming from inside that room
Let heavenly music resonate from inside that room
Let Amazing Grace be sung inside that room
Let gratitude be expressed inside that room."

I prayed, "Lord, if it is that room, then
Let fragmented relationships be mended in that room
Let broken marriages be reconciled in that room
Let lonely people find companionship in that room
Let disturbed minds find relaxation in that room
Let sick bodies be healed in that room
Let those who mourn be comforted in that room."

I said, "God, if it is that room, then
Let freedom reign within that room
Drive out all fear within that room
Let depressive thoughts be diminished within that room
Let lives shackled in chains of sin be released, within that room
Let impure thoughts be mortified within that room
Let love be demonstrated within that room."

"Lord, if it is that room, then
Let backbiters and talebearers not be entertained in that room
Let hypocrites feel uneasy in that room
Let domestic violence find zero tolerance in that room
Let hatred be crushed in that room
Let envy and jealousy be exterminated in that room
Let God the Father, Son, and Holy Spirit feel welcome in that room."

"God, if it is that room, then
Let credible security clearance be accepted inside that room
Let transparency be demonstrated inside that room
Let tax returns be submitted inside that room
Let democracy be practiced inside that room
Let executive privileges not be abused inside that room
Let no one think they are above the law inside that room."

"Lord, if it is that room, then
Let not egomaniacs, antisocial psychopaths, and demoniacs
Be allowed inside that room
Let not liars who are economical with the truth
Be subpoenaed inside that room
Let not alcoholic beverages be consumed inside that room
Let not recreational drugs be experimented with, inside that room
Let not profanity be spoken inside that room
Prohibit sexual temptations and illicit sexual practices inside that
room."

"Father, if it is that room, then
Let soft answers be spoken within that room
Let forgiveness and mercy be extended within that room
Let guilt and shame be overcome within that room
Let purity, chastity, and integrity be cherished within that room
Let good stewardship be practiced within that room
Let Satan be defeated within that room.

"Lord, if it is that room, then
Transform that room from the loft-type room, to The Upper Room
Let destiny be changed in The Upper Room
Let prodigal sons and daughters return home, to The Upper Room
Let disciples for Christ be made in The Upper Room
Let saints be sealed for God's kingdom, in The Upper Room
Let Jesus reign supreme, in The Upper Room."

"God, if it is that room, then
Favor her with The Upper Room
Work miracles inside that room
Let manna from heaven be served inside that room
Let the poor, the homeless, outcasts, and immigrants
Receive help inside that room
Supply every need in that room
Thank you, God, for providing that room
That very room, the Loft-type room
The Upper Room!

———⁓⁓⁓⁓———

# Adventism Is Moving On

Over A Hundred Years Ago
On Grenada's Beautiful Shore
Arrived The Advent Message
Wrapped Up In A Brilliant White Package
Delivered By Pastor Coon
Light! Now Penetrated The Gloom

You See
Darkness Had Covered The Land
And Gross Darkness The Local People
Practicing Obeah Was The Thing To Do
Chasing Largabless, Fighting Ligaroo
Immortality Of The Soul
Was Widely Believed By Both Young And Old

On Sunday, They Went To Church To Pray
Saturday Was The Market Day
Common Law Living Did Not Matter
Cheating, Cursing, Stealing From Each Other,
Drinking Strong Rum Was No Cause For Alarm
Or Eating Blood Pudding, Bacon, And Ham

One Hundred Years Along
Adventism Is Moving Strong
The Grenada Conference Has Been Established
Organizing God's Work, Taking Care Of His Business

To Pastor Punch We Give Recognition
As The First President Of The Grenada SDA Mission
Pastor Lewis, The Next Conference President
Leads The Workforce With Enthusiasm And Commitment
Churches Are On Fire, With Jesus Their Master
On The Battlefield, Conquering And To Conquer
Sauteurs, Chantimelle, Grand Roy, Victoria
Snell Hall, Paradise, Westerhall, Maranatha

The Coming Of Jesus Is Preached With Conviction
Redemption In Christ, Only Hope Of Salvation
Observe The Sabbath On Saturday
Is The Loud Cry Given From Day To Day
Babylon Is Rotten, "Come Out!" Is The Call
On Judgment Day, She Will Surely Fall

The Health Message Is Urgent And Clear
Give Up The Cigarette; Stop Drinking The Beer
Hypertension, Diabetes, All Types Of Cancer
Are Killing Our People, Left, Right, And Center
The Medical Mission Drives That Volunteers Engage In
Provide Health Education And Various Types Of Screening

One Hundred Years From Now
Adventism Will Likely Be Gone
The Bridegroom Would Have Come
To Take His Loved Ones Home
God's People No Longer Prone To Sin
The Devil's Been Destroyed, His Followers With Him

In The Land Where We'll Never Grow Old
We Will Walk The Streets Of Gold
Eating From The Tree Of Life
Building Mansions, What A Glorious Sight

Our Crowns Will Sparkle With Jewels Bright
With Jesus The Light, There'll Be No Night
Our Sabbath Service Will Remain
We Will Worship Jesus, The Lamb That Was Slain
That Same Jesus Who Liberated Our Spice Island
Over a Hundred Years Ago
Will Continue His Walk Beside Us
Now And Forevermore.

# Christians, Watch

Watch out! Christian soldier,
Trust in your Creator
Know Jesus as your Savior
Think thoughts that are purer
Let your light shine brighter
Strive not for power
Run the race with fervor
And watch! Unto prayer

Watch out! Christian soldier,
Honor your father and mother
Be an obedient son or daughter
A good brother or sister
Respect your elder
Be a good listener
Control your anger
And watch! Unto prayer

Watch out! Christian soldier,
Don't disrespect your pastor
Be kind to your neighbor
Embrace that mean church member
Forgive your offender
Give to that poor beggar
Feed those suffering from hunger
And watch! Unto prayer

Watch out! Christian soldier,
Have a sense of humor
Enjoy some good old laughter
Don't just strive to be popular
Or pride yourself in being peculiar
Watch your speedometer
Be gentle on the accelerator
And watch! Unto prayer

Watch out! Christian soldier,
Drink eight glasses of water
Avoid too much salt and sugar
Fasting will help you think clearer
Exercise will make you feel better
Enjoy the things of nature
Get enough rest and slumber
Be a faithful Sabbath keeper
And what I say unto you
I say unto all, "watch!
Watch unto prayer!"

# Just for Me

It was a long, agonizing prayer
The disciples couldn't stay awake any longer
He'd asked them to watch with Him
But then, He was taken from them
Taken from Gethsemane
Tied up and hurried off
Sent to the High Priest's palace
Interrogated
Disowned by His good friend and follower, Peter
Mocked in Pilate's judgment hall
Crowned with entwined thorns pierced deep into His skull
Stripped of His clothes
Dressed and mocked in a kingly purple robe
Dethroned and demoted from "King of Kings" to "King of the Jews"
Slapped in the face, ridiculed
Spat upon
Sent to death row to be crucified on a cross
Struggled carrying the cross to Golgotha
A Black man helped carry the cross
Nailed, stripped of His clothes and dignity
No privacy
Cross thrown violently in a hole
What pain and agony that must be
He asked for a drink
Was dehydrated, hungry, and thirsty
Offered a piece of sponge soaked in vinegar

No water to offer
But horrible-tasting vinegar
"God," He said, "why have You forsaken Me?"
Silence!
No reply from the Father
Psychological torture
But the Father was beside Him
Enshrouded in the darkness, hurting
Jesus died of a broken heart
As if that wasn't enough
Physical torture followed in death
Stabbed with a spear in His side to make sure he was dead
Really dead, completely dead
Blood and water poured out
How could that be?
Yes, the blood that was shed for you and me
He did it for you, for me
Behold, Calvary

# I Will Arise

I will arise and go to my Father and say,
"Father, here I am, your poor wretched child
Hopeless, and in need of your grace, your favor
I am not worthy to be called your child
I am a sinner
Cold, wretched, helpless sinner
Your prodigal child
I am undeserving of your love, your mercy
Your generosity, your pity
You taught me better
But upon impulse, in rage, in anger
I demanded my portion of what I felt was my entitlement
My entitlement to your hard earned savings
Your investments, your retirement money
Your 401K
I left your home, my comfortable home
I squandered your money
I threw everything down the gutter, until
In utter despair, I was left alone
Left alone to be beaten and battered
Beaten, battered, by the harsh elements of the weather
Scorching heat by day
Bone-chilling cold by night
Fierce, fiery lightning and roaring thunder

My so-called friends had deserted me
They were all gone, disappeared in thin air
Insect bites decorated my dry, fragile skin
My face emaciated, ghostly pale and thin
Thirst and hunger raged within
Sleepless nights caused me to hallucinate
As if I was seeing my dead mother dancing in front of heaven's gate
What a terrible state
But gladly I ate from the pigs' plate
In order to escape the pangs of death
Then last night, I saw a man
He stood in front of me. I was stunned
Clothed in the whitest garment I'd ever seen
His eyes like fiery flame
His woolen hair as white as snow
His mouth as sharp as a two-edged sword
He beckoned me to come to Him
He pointed toward the way I had walked years ago
That familiar road away from home
Where at the intersection
I crossed over toward the flashing lights of the big enticing city."
"Child, go back home," the man said to me.
"You have wasted your substance, nothing left, see."
My mind was tortured
I could stand it no longer
"So here I come, my beloved Father
But not as Your child, but a total stranger
I indulged in sin, though I knew much better
For You taught me to stay away from the pigs and the gutter
So now I come, not as Your son or daughter
But as Your hired servant in the midst of my storm
Can't delay much longer, the storm is over

Forgive me, dear Father
Here I am
I surrender
I surrender, all!"

# Christ, the Solid Rock

Oh people of this congregation,
In this world of sin and degradation
We have arrived at the conclusion
And there is no doubt in our cognition
That Jesus Christ is our solid Rock foundation

From the time of His incarnation
To the day of His dedication
He was a child of divine admiration
Filled with heavenly inspiration

Throughout His earthly ministration, crucifixion, and resurrection
Until the day of His coronation
He was driven by determination to secure man's salvation
Oh people of this congregation

Oh people of this congregation,
During the judgment investigation
The Prince of execution
Will perform the separation of His chosen generation
Providing their qualification meet with God's approbation
Through justification and sanctification

Oh people of this congregation,
When we see earth's desolation
Foretold by prophetic revelation, unfolds its wings of destruction

And as we experience tribulation
The impending translation will be our only consolation
As we await Christ's second visitation

Oh people of this congregation,
It is beyond our imagination
To understand God's magnificent preparation
Of our spectacular glorification
When we shall have arrived at our destination

Oh people of this congregation,
Ever more with joy and adoration
We shall join with all peoples, tongues, and nations
The saved of God's creation
With our robes of purification
Our crowns of exaltation
And our harps of acclamation
Resounding songs of liberation
Resounding songs of liberation
Resounding songs of liberation
Worshipping the Rock of our Salvation
From Genesis to Revelation
Forever, forever, and ever.
Amen.

# Thanks

Thanks for Your grace, Your saving grace
For keeping us safe from the destruction we face
Your unconditional love, You demonstrate
Your great sacrifice for the human race

For giving us a home, to lay our head
For providing us with, our daily bread
For hearing our groans, for alleviating our pain
For wiping our tears, when loved ones are slain

For being our Comforter, in the thick of the storm
For forgiving our sins, when we've done You wrong
For the promises You've given, in the Word of Life
For providing us protection, from our daily strife

For family, for loved ones, friends, and neighbors too
For health and strength, to face life's many battle
Thanks for Your faithfulness, oh God our Father
Help us to serve You wholeheartedly, forever!

THANKS!

# Kingdom Quiz

Find in your Bible each of the above kingdom reminders!
Place the correct Scripture next to each one.
Give three points for each correct response.

# Kingdom Prayer

Our Father in heaven,
may your name always be kept holy.
May your kingdom come
and what you want be done,
here on earth as it is in heaven.
Give us the food we need for each day.
Forgive us for our sins,
just as we have forgiven those who sinned against us.
And do not cause us to be tempted,
but save us from the Evil One.
[The kingdom, the power, and the glory are yours forever. Amen.]
(see Matt. 6:9–13, NCV).